Call and Response

Conversations in Verse

Call and Response

Conversations in Verse

poems by

Jack B. Bedell

and

Darrell Bourque

Texas Review Press
Huntsville, Texas
A Member of the Texas A&M Press Consortium

FIRST EDITION, 2009

Cover Art: Glorio Fiero, *Arnaudville*, courtesy of the artist.

Cover Image photographed by Philip Gould

Darrell Bourque Author's Photo: Philip Gould

Requests for permission to reproduce material from this work should be sent to:

Texas Review Press
English Department
Sam Houston State University
P.O. Box 2146
Huntsville, TX 77341-2146

Library of Congress Cataloging-in-Publication Data

Bedell, Jack, 1966-
   Call and response : conversations in verse / Jack B. Bedell and Darrell Bourque.
     p. cm.
   ISBN 978-1-933896-40-3 (alk. paper)
   I. Bourque, Darrell. II. Title.
   PS3552.E2877C35 2009
   811'.54--dc22

                          2009032046

Contents

Acknowledgments

Very grateful acknowledgment is made to the editors of the following journals where many of these poems first appeared:

Connecticut Review: "A Barn in Arnaudville" and "Bougalie"
Connecticut River Review: "My Son Discovers the Draw of Water"
The Hudson Review: "Elvin Jones at Midnight," "George Foreman in Zaire," and "The Injury Wall"
Interdisciplinary Humanities: "Egret Haiku" and "Cane Field Haiku"
Paddlefish: "*The Artist and His Model*, Matisse 1919," "Proof: That Space and Time Do Intersect," and "Waitfulness"
Texas Review: "Django Reinhardt at *La Cigale*," "The Geese on Hwy. 16," and "Saturday Night Crab Boils"
TriQuarterly: "Family Album"
Vineyards: "Monet's *La Pie*"

"One Day, Working" was featured on *www.TheRumpus.net*.

"*The Artist and His Model*, Matisse 1919" also appeared in the *Alambra Poetry Calendar 2009*.

"A Barn in Arnaudville" will appear in the *Alambra Poetry Calendar 2010*.

"My Son Discovers the Draw of Water" was reprinted in Negative Capability Press' anthology *Whatever Remembers Us* and in the Yale Medical Group's *Caduceus, Vol. 6*.

"One Day, Working" and "Waitfulness" were reprinted in the Yale Medical Group's *Caduceus, Vol. 5*.

Authors' Preface

Growing up in south Louisiana, I've been bitten by thousands of mosquitoes. It's happened so many times, in fact, that I've always thought of bug bites as a natural part of life, like breathing and sleeping. It's funny to me now that one of those bites would change my life so drastically.

In the spring of 2006, I contracted West Nile virus, though I didn't know it at the time, and wouldn't until being diagnosed in early fall. Over the course of several months, the virus invaded my nervous system, and I developed a variety of symptoms—profound fatigue, muscle cramping and twitching, and a strange kind of roving numbness.

Between the physical problems brought on by the infection and my own anxiety over what was happening to me, I was able to do little more than sit around the house or the office obsessing over new symptoms. I couldn't find a way to enjoy simple pleasures in my life like holding my sons or walking with my wife, and I definitely couldn't focus enough to write.

When this apathy lasted into the new year, I knew I needed something to pull me out of the bog I was in. I had medicines helping me with physical symptoms, but I really needed someone to help me make poems again, because I knew that was the quickest way to jumpstart my heart and get me back into life.

That's when I wrote Darrell asking him to do this project with me. I had no idea how to go about things, how to truly collaborate on a book of poems. I just knew Darrell Bourque was the person I had always wanted to be from the first day I met him, so caring and talented and in life, and if anyone could draw me back to the things that were important to me, it would be Darrell.

The poems in *Call and Response* are a record of that drawing out. Whether calling or responding, I had to stretch my ideas of what a poem could be and how it might be framed to match Darrell's abilities. That reaching made me excited again, and in Darrell's debt. I hope you enjoy the results as much as I have.

—Jack B. Bedell

Poetry is for me one form of conversation. It is a way of talking back and talking into things—talking back and talking into memory, and ancestry; talking into the geographies I inhabit and the family I am part of; talking back at calamity and experience; talking into relationship, talking back and talking into the languages that have shaped my understanding of the world I live in; talking back and talking into history; talking into possibility and into hope.

I believe strongly that what we do as poets is but a variant of what the musician does, what the historian does, what the storyteller does, what the painter and what the sculptor does and what film makers do. My work as a poet relies on interdependence. I write in solitude but my work is not solitary. I am partner at one time with painters in whose work I see poems, in other times with composers' works in which I hear the lines of poems, even in critical pieces containing the language of poetry. For me poetry is a conversation in which there is no breach between the political and the personal, between the cultural and the individual. And for me this conversation is a vital one.

This kind of artful conversation is not new at all. It resides in the ekphrastic work of Homer who responds to the work of the goldsmith Hephaestus when he describes Achilles' shield in *The Iliad*. Since that early call and response poem in the epic many writers have written in this tradition and it is a popular contemporary genre of poetry.

Lady Murasaki was following a time-honored tradition in Japanese poetry when she included nearly 800 poetic responses in her classic Heian culture novel of eleventh-century Japan. Murasaki believed it was the mark of the uncultured and the barbaric to encounter art or the artful and have no response: "It was unthinkable that a poem should get no reply (*The Tale of Genji*)." Other highly formalized poetry traditions and rituals of Japan emerge in practices of the linked-verse poetry of *renga* where a group of poets gather in a formal setting to work for hours or even days composing a collaborative poem. We are not startled to find poems inscribed on the visual texts of Oriental screens, scrolls, and paintings or to see poems which have been created in response to some painter's work.

Closer to our own poets we find William Carlos Williams and W. H. Auden responding to the country wedding dance and to Icarus' falling in two of Brugel's memorable paintings. It is not unusual to see poets honoring or acknowledging other poets in their own poems. Take, for instance, Pound's homage to as unlikely a paired poet as Whitman.

Integral to Southern American culture is the call and response of work songs which accompanied the work in the fields and on construction sites. This kind of artful conversation is recorded as well in the songs of the track liners who created America's railroads. Related to these kinds of responsorials is the kind of exchange that takes place in religious ritual and ceremony, which I encountered growing up Catholic in litanies, novenas, the ritual of The Way of the Cross, and the congregational responses of Requiems and High Mass. The role of the responsorial is connected to "audience" response, designated or otherwise, which adds richness and texture to medieval poems. Response seems not only natural but at the heart of the poetic impulse as I know it and have worked within it for all my life.

So, when Jack wrote to ask me to write with him on this new project he had in mind, it felt right and natural to be working in this tradition. Even more exciting for me was the knowledge that I would be working with a master poet who has a distinctive and definitive stamp of his own in every poem of his I have read. I knew that we worked often in different styles and forms but that our voices would feel right in this engagement. To be asked to sing with a master singer is something that does not happen for many poets and so I was both pleased and humbled in accepting the challenge and launching the project.

—Darrell Bourque

NOTE TO READERS—*Call and Response* begins with Darrell Bourque's "Durer's Meditation on Small Things: *The Great Piece of Turf, 1503*" to which Jack Bedell's "*The Artist and His Model*, Matisse, 1919" responds. The rest of the collection follows this alternation.

Call and Response

Conversations in Verse

For Beth
and
For Karen

DÜRER'S MEDITATION ON SMALL THINGS:
THE GREAT PIECE OF TURF, 1503

It is the composition I am forever walking by
moves me most when I finally stop to look.
What is it turning us outside ourselves, what hook
hooks us and pulls us from whatever sky

we have come to inhabit as though we love
there and only there? It is a switch
after all, this hook. It shifts horizons. Heavy mauve

the sky can be is eclipsed by something as neatly stitched
as this little patch of earth. I have measured what moved
me here, this patch is small by any standard but so rich

we could get lost in this country of green if we were to try.
A small golden ribbon of a snake, you ask. It is your book
to read. Crested dandelion stems, landscapes of crooked
grasses. What my eye loved I made for your eye.

The Artist and His Model, Matisse, 1919

—for my wife who is more than love

There's never been a hand more versed
in the way light curves around beauty,
how color cushions life day by day,
than his, yet here's Matisse stiff as iron,

his spine so straight the stripes of his pajamas
could almost cut their way off the canvas.
Not three feet away, a sumptuous nude reclines
in the most comfortable armchair ever painted,
the lines of her body at peace, the room around her

aromatic and brewing slowly like spiced tea.
Flowers lean. A table cloth pours
like honey onto pink tile. The air,
full of sea salt, glows gold and warm.

The artist, though, is cold at work, his brush
poised but not painting a thing, his canvas
so empty and joyless it makes my chest ache
with fear it may never fill, that he might never
see himself in all this richness.

Across the room, my wife's on one knee
putting a sweatshirt on our youngest boy,
his smile so big it could swallow the heavy sun
flooding in from the backdoor glass.

In the kitchen, our crab stew thickens on the stove,
garlic rolls rise through the house and settle
somewhere near my soul. I close the book,
take one deep breath to let it go, and slouch
so far into the couch I could easily be a lost coin.

LETTER FROM LEBANON

—for Faraj Farajalla

first line from Aga Shahid Ali's "Homage to Faiz Ahmed Faiz"

You wrote this from Beirut, two years before
you finally left for good. You said your losses
were almost more than you could bear, scores
of friends had to flee, aunts and uncles tossed

like trees in a storm that never let up. Waving
goodbye was as incessant as waves in the sea
you played in as a child. The moon's paving

a road in water, the only road you could be
on in those nights. You had to take what they gave.
You had to pretend to like it until you could freeze

your heart. Bombs shattered and shifted more
than stores and houses. In churches crosses
toppled and fell. Blood, gasoline, and hatred poured.
Gardeners torched roses, cedars, scorched the mosses.

George Foreman in Zaire

—for Norman Mailer, who would know

Achilles never showed up to a fight
to find some other half-god like Hercules
geared up and fighting for the other side.
He beat down his honorable Hectors,
stared away his wicked kings,
and piled up his laurels without equal
until he found himself lying in the grass of Troy
unable to breathe and dying,
an arrow from some coward's bow
having found his one weakness
from a hundred yards away.
Fate spared him the pain of getting up,
of living past that cold night, of age.

Staring up into a wet African sky, though,
Foreman knew he'd have to get up,
eventually, take off his gloves,
and walk past Ali raising his belt,
past a stronger man with better anger than his own.
And as much as he must have wished
for some succubus to blame
or some blueprint of fate to excuse his loss,
he had felt the worth of another man
pressed right up against his body
and had found the weight

impossible to bear. It was enough
to take his breath away, I'm sure,
but like the rest of us, suddenly,
he lifted himself up,
and his feet found the ground.

SCRATCH

Since that afternoon years ago
when my mother put us on our knees
and told us she was leaving,
I have placed myself in the world,
measured myself against the horizon,
let the sky cover me like some angel bird
hovering. I have seen wide ribbons
of pine making a trot-line at the earth's edge.
I have studied things up-close: stunted trees
growing out of rock. I have gone beyond
tree lines where grasses open seedpods
like prayers. I have stood at the water's
edge and wobbled, and still no one
knows who knifed the unreadable lettering
on my mother's new cedar chifferobe
that day. She and my father drove to town
to buy garfish for our usual Friday supper
at my aunt's house. We were questioned again
on her return but no one confessed –through
the fish cleaning, the seasoning, the frying.
I can't remember when exactly we laughed
and ran through the yard with our cousins.
It was night when we went home. We were happy.
Just last week, some fifty years later,
one of us brings it up in my mother's
presence. She has not walked for years

and it is no big matter to her now,
but none of us are fessing up today either.
We all know who didn't do it,
and one of us knows who did.

The Injury Wall

My mother had no use for subtlety.
Her lessons came without parable,
without nagging hints or leading questions
to herd us toward the light. If she wanted
our feet off the coffee table, she gave us one chance,
then kicked them off herself. If she thought the girl
I'd brought home was split-tail and a waste of time,
she said so before any food was served,
no need to put work into a lost cause.

To teach us the brutal truth of pain,
she had the injury wall. When my father or brother
came home bloodied or broken, she'd back them up
against our living room wall, right in front
of the cypress shelf that held what was left
of the china figurines she'd kept before us,
and snap a Polaroid before they'd get
any doctoring. The pictures testified
to all the history of hurt we'd seen—

my father burned and hairless from a rig fire
so hot it melted away the black stone
from his Masonic ring, my brother skinned raw
from running his motorcycle into the neighbor's house,
the flathead screwdriver in his pocket mistaken
for a broken rib, the boy from next door

who'd torn an ear when we pitched him
off the roof into our magnolia bush.
Only the photographer and I were absent.

It wasn't that I was such a good student,
or that luck shined on me in any way
to keep me off the wall. It's just my pain
was never skin-deep or photogenic
enough to rate pulling the camera down.
A broken collarbone here, some cracked ribs there,
a heart left behind by some *jolie blonde*.
Truth is, I still lie awake some nights
conjuring scrapes, pulling scars to the surface
ugly enough to earn me a spot on the wall,
wondering what my mother would say about that.

QUIETISM

—first line from Naomi Shihab Nye's "Walking Down Blanco Road at Midnight"

It happens in a quiet place.
If too much is moving around,
you never get to see the thin line
of red flickering above the horizon
just before sunrises or just after
sunset – some tag of fire or herald
of no sound whatsoever.
There is a moment when all leave
the table but something still breathes
as fat congeals on plates left behind.
The big chair in the yard near the oak
lived in the silence of trees in forests.
The tools put up in the winter shed,
silent in their work and in their rest.
An audiologist's finest instrument
might never record the calla lily's
slow, long, unfolding song.

Waitfulness

—first line from Mark Jarman's "The Wind"

Worried about the children I kept waiting
after every noise that pulled me from sleep,

waiting in the thick quiet for some flicker
of security to give me back my breath,

until I realized there is no peace
like the moments of silence between a child's cry

and the sound of quick feet running
toward your bed, the rush of cold air

when the duvet lifts and a small body wedges
into the space you give it, the warmth next to you

like a sunrise, the sleep rich as forest growth,
the wait turning every breath into song.

LOVESICK: FROM LESBOS TO NASHVILLE

"The moon just went behind a cloud
To hide its face and cry"
—from "I'm So Lonesome I Could Cry" The Hank Williams' Songbook

Sappho, trans. Mary Barnard

(§ 37 *You know the place: then*)

I prayed you would
come to me. I tried
to lure you with murmuring
of streams in stands
of apple trees.
You were with someone else
you could not leave.
Bees made music for you
in your own lemon grove
in Crete.

(§ 39 *He is more than a hero*)

I tried and tried to tell you
how I could not speak
if I met you suddenly.
I tried to move you, even
with a broken tongue.
A thin flame, I told you then,
runs under my skin.
Well, today blood
could hardly be said to run.
A wafting of ashes
there instead; sick birds
struggling in the lightest
winds.

(§ 42 *I have not heard one word from her*)

All that talk about unwilling
parting, all that poetry
about our gifts to Aphrodite,
how you melted me
in that sad hour
with sung apologies.
You could not leave,
you said, without reminding
me "*no voices chanted
choruses without ours,
no woodlot bloomed in spring with-
out song ...*"
I hung on your every word,
asked you only to remember
who you left hobbled.
It is no wonder
*the moon just went behind a cloud
to hide its face and cry.*

(§   45   *If you will come*)

I shall put out
new [skin] *for*
you to rest on

(§   63   *Last night*)

I dreamed [...]
You and I had
words: Cyprian

My skin crawled—

(§   87   *We know this much*)

Death is an evil;
we have the gods'
word for it; they too
would die if death
were a good thing

When you left,
it was like death.

Birds of ash
in the lemon
grove had no song.
They were not nightingales,
did not know what to do
in a world unlighted.
The hours could
weigh heavily,
or could not.
It was nothing to them.
Someone slipped the knot
of gravity.

It was like death.
We know this much.

Elvin Jones at Midnight

There are nights when I have complete control
of the stereo, nights when I can put on Coltrane
without my wife's face dropping into a frown.

Those nights, I can step to the back door
with the inexcusable pleasure of Elvin Jones
harassing the snare with his left hand,

tickling more sound out of his cymbals
than any one limb should be able to get,
and kicking just enough ahead of the beat

to make the whole band chase his time.
There's an undertone of harmony
in Jones' kit I know I'll have to explain

to my sons one day, hopefully in moonlight,
hopefully soon. I'll load them into the golf cart
with drinks and clubs and a jam box, take them

out onto the ninth green behind our house
and let them loose to do whatever damage they can
out of earshot of their mother. I'll play

the music for them, tell them it's the same sound
my blood makes going through my ears, hoping
they'll listen long enough to understand

before one of them asks me to shut off the noise,
or to put on something with words in it,
before I'll have to tell them it's the words
that mess things up sometimes.

THE ARUM LILIES IN MY MOTHER'S DREAM

My mother says he looks like he just stepped out
of a photograph in this visitation. This man, my father,
is wearing a blue seersucker suit and a red tie.

This is the man who never wore a blue anything
and he never owned a red tie. But he is here
in her dream. He barely speaks in this apparition.

He pushes his chair from the table, gets up
and stands for a moment seeming to admire
the arum lilies she's brought in from the garden.

She could not have told if he had any feeling at all
for flowers. He seldom said what he liked. A moment
only, then these flowers and then he says he has to go.

Bougalie

My marraine says she still has dreams
of walking to the English school

afraid because she has no words
for the *croûte de pain* and *étouffée*

she's brought for lunch, knowing she'll kneel
on rice for hours, or worse be sent

to march around the flag pole
with one red brick in each hand

while blonde *teteuxs* from in front the class
giggle and sing songs about her.

She says these dreams last for days,
useless like food on the tongue, unswallowed.

When she wakes, her knuckles ache
so fierce it takes her most of the morning

to lay her fingers straight, and longer
before her knees feel right for walking.

EGRET HAIKU

Rising from grasses,
egrets in the farthest field,
spume on a green wave.

Egrets in rice fields,
I sew this year's kimono--
spring flight in green silk.

Egrets follow close
to my tractor in the field--
they love grubs I turn.

In midsummer light
we hardly see the egrets--
white enlightenment.

A flock of egrets
turn sharply back to the earth--
love turns on itself.

Egrets on branches
in trees in the rookeries,
white autumn tree lace.

In winter ditches
egrets and equisetum--
yellow and green sprouts..

Whole flocks of egrets
stitched into a large, thick quilt--
I dream white bird dreams.

Cane Field Haiku

Smoke above cane fields,
white tablecloths for the fête,
sun settles on fall.

Under bright moonlight,
lovers lie beneath blankets.
Beside them cane grows.

Red hawks skim the rows,
king snakes slink toward winter,
the cane lives at night.

Between the tall stalks,
rabbits and coons hide from flames,
nice meat for our stew.

Fire spreads through the fields
from inside out, leaving all black.
Kids play in the smoke.

Cane brulée standing,
the real work is left for dawn,
stalks for the cutters.

Lost fingers and pain,
sweet sugar comes at a price.
Some things don't grow back.

Cut cane brought to mill,
old dresses are put away,
a new year's fresh hope.

ON AN OVERGROWN PATH

—after Leoš Janáček
for Karen

The red table still holds its redness
after all these years. It is chairless
now, this table we took our meals on.
But the lilies you planted in the borders
still bloom every month as you planned
it. Spider lilies in September, arum lilies
throughout the summer, amaryllis in
the early spring and crocuses and tulips
and hyacinths in their time. Nun's
orchids are still here among the weeds
and grasses as is the evergreen wisteria
with Zéphirine Drouhin roses twining
through it, dropping petals in our plates.
And we are here too, surveyors upright
and open, in the tangle we still tend.

One Day, Working

—after Ted Kooser
for Beth

Last Saturday, we spent the afternoon
tending to the garden we'd left too long
on its own. While the children played half-naked
in the yard shooting the hose pipe at anything
that moved, I fought the lawless hedges,
and you pulled blackberry vines. I am certain
there were green snakes coiled in the branches
near your fingers, or hornet's nests throbbing
from all our work, that would have scattered us
back to a day of bills or cleaning inside.
But on this day, the boys ran in the water,
the dog rolled in the grass, and you
stood there glowing in the June sun,
all floral and sweet as a breath to be taken.

HOLLYBEACH, 1952

I was ten when my parents brought me to the beach for the first time,
and it was somewhat hard to tell what of this greyish brown was sand
and what was water. There was clearly something happening in the line
where the horizon was supposed to be, some curve I knew from land

and how it met the sky. I was not completely unfamiliar with rhymes
the earth itself teaches the young who look and measure, with strands
that finally knit themselves into some kind of rope of meaning, fine
distinctions that merge into larger being. But I had never had to stand

by myself before something I could walk into like this, could climb
into, it seemed to me, as the gulf shaped itself into this bulge, a grand
stilled opacity that did not even look like water. I had surely primed
myself to bravery as parents and aunts and cousins and sisters fanned

behind me in their own play. But when the water finally surged around me,
I was ten, could never have imagined such rotary or how to hold a dizzy sea.

My Son Discovers the Draw of Water

—Samuel, Gulf Shores, 2005

He was still getting used to the sand between his toes
        when the cool Gulf water crashed around his thighs,
                knocking him back, then drawing him closer to home.

It took barely a second for his face
        to go from complaint to laughter, for him to feel
                the rhythm of the tide, to taste the salt

splashing his smile. Three steps forward, two steps
        back. Again and again. All light and love.
                It wasn't until the water reached his chest

he realized this was more than a game of chase,
        more than simple joy, and that all pleasures
                come with a price. He turned to shore and cried

for us to bring him back to the heavy sand.

EINSTEIN'S VIOLIN

He lived in a world where things fell short,
and it was in that very world where he enlarged
everything we knew about its ways. His heart
would not abide lockstep of any kind. Charged

orders for him were thoughts so wild and untamed
the maths to chart them often wouldn't follow. He failed
at marriages and loves; one beloved son he named

Tete fell into holes that swallowed him. But he sailed
in hard times wherever he could find water, framed
grief and loss with yet another leap he shaped and nailed

into a poetry of physics—straight lines curve *en fin*, part
of a way to explain a universe no one could have carved
before him. Always by his side the violin, Bach & Mozart
to visit with: sound, a bright smile; memory, a line curved.

Proof: That Space and Time Do Intersect

(a)
The day passes, as many do,
a blur of student conferences
and six-dollar coffees to make it through
to the weekend where time slows down
for soccer games, birthday parties,
cartoons, and football.
                              My two-mile drive
to the house at 45 miles per hour
takes the same 15 minutes,
inexplicably. The same amount
of time it takes to shake off all thoughts
of work and duties and things undone.

(b)
Then, variables:

                              My parents' car
in the driveway, unexpectedly,
the garage colder than it's been all year.

Inside, the house is warm and I'm met
with a smell I remember as long as any
in my life.
                   My mom is at the stove
sautéing onions, peppers, and celery.

The butter crackles in the pot, contagious
like a smile that bends around every corner
of the room.
                    My wife looks over her shoulder
to learn how she browns her roux just right
for gumbo.
                    Outside in the sun, my sons
are playing chase all over the yard.
Laughing, fighting, crying, laughing.
I don't even need to see them to know
they are holding each other and rolling in the grass.

My dad is on the sofa watching the news.
My sofa, the same news, our dog curled up
at his feet like a thought he can't shake.

(c)
From the spot in the den where I drop my book bag,
I can see it all. If I close my eyes,
I am 6 again, then 30, then 3, then 41.
Time folds, contracts, expands, glows
through the backdoor glass.
                    My heart beats
and life is syncopated, unexpectedly,
inexplicably in time with itself.

DÜRER'S *POND IN THE WOODS*

In Dürer's brush no one is surprised by loss
or plenty. The trees on the left are but shafts
of what they once were. Under them mosses
spill through rocks and grasses. He's drafted

a little beach on the other side. A white
triangle at the foot of a stand of fir
or some other conifer. Here, one might

imagine lovers emerging or saints stirred
by waves of passion. Here, the inky night
suggested by dark water & clouds perturbed

in a golden sky are but another jostling
of light and dark, an allegory he's crafted
in paint. Everywhere there is murk and dross.
Everywhere there is to everything light grafted.

Monet's *La Pie*

The bird sits there on the rack, as black
      and literal as the word against white page,
            unavoidable. Everything else

is covered in snow, shades of light, tans,
      greys, degrees of white. The things we know
            are there beneath the ice we have to take

on faith—the rough-hewn fence in the foreground,
      the roof of the farmhouse behind, branches of hardwoods
            stretching all the way back to the horizon line.

Yet we know they are there, incarnate
      and solid, heavy as that tiny, black bird,
            begging at the edges of our soul.

THE HAND OF THOUGHT

We have this notion about the roads we walk
on. We think that if we should cross a bridge
once, it will be there to cross again. We stalk
regularity and sameness; we want the ridge

we covered yesterday to be the one seam
we can rely on forever. We want the window's
in our houses to give us steady beams

of light. In autumn we want yellow indoor
light to fall softly on the carpets, the creams
and reds and blues hardly disturbed. Winter

light will be dense and heavy, table weight. Talk,
but nothing to do us in. Something in us cringes
at the thought of running into things and we bark
at anything – boulders, leaves, swarms of midges.

The Geese on Hwy. 16

I took Hwy. 16 north out of town
   for the first time the other day. Not two miles out
the flat, piney land I'd lived in
   for a decade and a half turned to rolling hills,

sweet grass and dairy farms on both sides of the road,
   like nothing else in Louisiana, treeless
and filled with black and white Guernseys
   lolling around cow ponds, haystacks,

red barns in the distance. Every hill I topped
   offered a scene off a butter box,
complete with farmhouse and green tractor.
   I couldn't help but feel I'd taken a wrong turn, somewhere.

Then unexpectedly the road crooked east,
   and every foot of pasture land as far
as I could see was covered with geese,
   Canada geese, each a yard tall and big around

as my six year old son. Most were grazing,
   but some seemed on guard, honking and watching
the road for what might pass occasionally.
   At the bottom of a hill, I slowed my truck

just to try a rough count. I looked
        ten by ten until I confused myself.
There were hundreds, maybe thousands,
        of these geese, so loud and out of place

I had to pull off the road to shake my head
        and laugh. What a heck of a morning it must have been
for the farmer coming out on his porch at dawn,
        hot coffee and paper in hand, to find this flock had landed.

ON LISTENING TO SCHUBERT

It is mechanics of mind
that intrigues me most
in Schubert's Quintet, Opus 163,
all that initial creeping
necessary
for what is being
set up.
Grief underlies all
it tries to cover up.
In this geography, it matters
little if the sky is blue
with mares tails
or blue without,
if the sky
is the hot white
the sky becomes at noon
on clear summer days,
or a veiled
white sky
with thinly falling
snow.
Or slate,
or black with thunderheads,
or not.
We are mostly moved away
and not toward

anything,
the strings
our only
consolation.

Django Reinhardt at *La Cigale*

He's come to the stage late from gambling,
his stomach heavy with wine and steak,
but the German officers queued up to see him
don't mind the wait. They have champagne,
French women, and his guitar to make them happy.

He plays like a man lucky to be alive—
a jazz-playing, crippled gypsy
accompanied by a Jew and three blacks,
surrounded by Nazis in occupied Paris,
free beyond any logic, free to play.

His swing bubbles on the surface,
perfect for hugging and conversation,
laced with enough lines of *les Allemandes*
even the Führer would love to hear
a set of his "St. Louis Blues."

Yet as high as the violin climbs in the score,
or as quick and bright as his guitar runs,
he cannot escape the Manouche frown
underpinning it all, the thought
of a half million of his brothers starving

on moldy bread and rancid pork
in concentration camps only a few hundred miles

from this club, his music the same they'd play
on accordion given the life to do so,
his heart two places at once.

No matter how hard he tries, no matter
how many people smile at his work,
the notes his two good fingers free
from the fretboard of his guitar
will never make it to the border.

PHOTOGRAPH FOR MY FATHER, 1944

In this one photograph of my mother
with her first three children, I am three.
My father is in California. My mother
is beautiful in this new role she's in.
My older sister looks directly at the camera.
Her beauty is straight-ahead beauty.
My younger sister turns her face
to the side, her beauty devastatingly oblique,

then and now. I am blank-faced with loss.
We are all being shaped by the very gift
we are trying to get to him before he's shipped
out. He will fade differently for each of us.
He will come home. He will tend to us
in his quiet way. Each of us will go on.
I will put lilies on his grave at Eastertime.

Family Album

All the pictures my mother's saved over the years
are posed, nothing candid, no shots of the old man
in bliss, barbecueing in the August heat,
taking that first sip off a Falstaff can,
no pics of her in hot pants, full-throat laughing,
leaning against the door of their new Chrysler.

Every Polaroid she's held onto
looks like it should have a string attached
to its back that moves my arm towards the fireplace
they'd just put in the living room, or that bends
my brother at the waist to show off
the kitchen's new parquet when the string's pulled.

The dancing at crab boils, the stolen kisses,
the times my brother fixed my shirt collar
and put his arm around my shoulders at the bus stop—
these images are kept in conversations now,
passed around the table on Sundays like gumbo,
left to hang in the room like mist waiting for the sun.

FRIDAY NIGHT FISH FRY

We have all gathered under the oak tree
in the back yard. The fish is frying
in one black pot, and over on the other fire
is my aunt's courtboullion made from three
large catfish the men caught earlier in the day.
It is not dark yet, but the moon in the east
is a large yellow plate floating on the horizon.
Our two bay mares are sleeping under it.
What matters least is what we don't have
in this moment, anything withheld pales
in waves rising from those two black pots.

Saturday Night Crab Boils

By the time the kids came in from playing chase or four squares or horseshoes, the tables were already piled high with blue crab, potatoes, and corn. All of it steaming hot and full of pepper and lemon, right off the butane and out of the pots. The eating was straight noise, everybody cracking shells with the handles of butter knives, picking out meat, and telling stories over somebody else's beat. The women drank highballs in gold-rimmed glasses. The men pulled beers from salted ice in every kind of can you could imagine—Pabst Blue Ribbon, Schlitz, Pearl, Falstaff, Jax. Then in no time flat, the shells were rolled up in old newspaper and thrown into garbage cans outside, the tables were folded up, and somebody cranked up the music for the *fais do-do*. As soon as the eight-track came on, our folks danced like the garage was a V.F.W. hall. They turned up the Frankie Laine and spun each other out into the oyster-shelled driveway, right into the street sometimes, spinning and juking to "Where the Wild Goose Goes" and not caring who heard or saw or wasn't invited to the party. They made joy, and we watched. Our folks moved and laughed and sang like nothing had to be cleaned or put away, like Monday wasn't going to be hard for any one of them.

THE BLACK DOOR IN *ARNAUDVILLE*

—for Gloria Fiero

It might be what you don't see that most pleases
in this scene. There are possible banks everywhere
in this thick expanse of lively grassland. Water teases
a presence here and storms embed themselves in the charged air.

Beyond the darkest trees on the horizon whole families
may be filling sacks with choupique or handfishing for turtles.
Lovers could settle in away from us in that little cluster of trees

near the barn. But these are passing things. They startle
no one, mere skitterings to circumvent the black door of mysteries
opening the rusty tin-covered, white pyramid amidst all the marbled

life teeming here, a grave opening defying opening. No one sees
anything discernible beyond this dark plane. There is something there
we think or hope, but it invites nothing we can easily take comfort in, frees
nothing. Yet, it is the painter's gift to us, something the landscape has to bear.

A Barn in Arnaudville

It sits on the edge of pasture land, surrounded
by scrub brush and hardwoods, its doors swung wide open,
all black inside and calling across the fields
to horses at play and men fixing fence
so far away they lean into the horizon,
its offer still, cool shade and safety
from the afternoon storm brewing overhead.

Everything growing on this land responds
by bending toward its invitation, straining
in the breeze against the dirt to head towards shelter.
Tall grass swirls, and trees huddle
as close as they can around the barn's edges.
Inside, there's nowhere near the space to hold it all,
yet something in the darkness gives us hope.

About the Authors

Jack B. Bedell was born and raised in south Louisiana. He earned his B.A. and M.A. from Northwestern State University in Natchitoches before attending the University of Arkansas-Fayetteville, where he earned his M.F.A., and the University of Louisiana—Lafayette, where he earned his Ph.D.

Currently, Bedell is the Woman's Hospital Distinguished Professor in the Humanities at Southeastern Louisiana University where he also serves as editor of *Louisiana Literature* and director of Louisiana Literature Press. His most recent books are *Come Rain, Come Shine* (Texas Review Press) and *French Connections: A Gathering of Franco-American Poets* (LaLit Press).

He's also author of *What Passes for Love* and *At the Bonehouse*, both published by Texas Review Press (a member of the Texas A&M Press Consortium) and *Greatest Hits* (Pudding House Press). His recent work appears in the *Southern Review, Hudson Review, Connecticut Review, Paterson Literary Review, Texas Review, Southeast Review*, and other journals.

He and his wife Beth have three children, Jack, Jr., Samuel Eli, and Emma Louise.

Darrell Bourque is Professor Emeritus in English from University of Louisiana where he taught in the English Department and in the Interdisciplinary Humanities Program. During his career there he directed the Creative Writing Program, was the Friends of the Humanities Honor Professor, and served as the Head of the English Department. He also was the President of the National Association for Humanities Education and edited the journal *Interdiscipliinary Humanities*.

Bourque's books include *Plainsongs* published by Cross-Cultural Communications (1994), *The Doors Between Us* (the inaugural issue of Louisiana Literature's Chapbook Series-1997), *Burnt Water Suite*, Wings Press (1999), and *The Blue Boat*, The Center for Louisiana Studies (2004).

Bourque was appointed Poet Laureate of Louisiana in 2007 and again in 2009. He lives with his wife Karen, who is a glass artist, in rural St. Landry Parish and they have two children and six grandchildren who live in the Houma-Thibodaux area.